SURVIVING
HOMEWORK

SURVIVING HOMEWORK

REAL HELP FROM REAL KIDS

Tips from TEENS

STUDY SECRETS TO CURE YOUR HOMEWORK HEADACHES!

AMY NATHAN

DRAWINGS BY ANNE CANEVARI GREEN

The Millbrook Press
Brookfield, Connecticut

For Eric and Noah

Published by The Millbrook Press, Inc.
2 Old New Milford Road, Brookfield, Connecticut 06804

Library of Congress Cataloging-in-Publication Data
Nathan, Amy.
Surviving homework: tips from teens/Amy Nathan.
p. cm.
Includes index.
ISBN 1-56294-185-2 (lib. bdg.)
1. Homework—Juvenile literature. 2. Study skills—Juvenile
literature. I. Title.
LB1048.N37 1996
372.13'028'12—dc20   95-40655 CIP AC

CONTENTS

HELP
IS ON THE WAY

Homework—a word that's greeted with moans, groans, gripes, and grumbles. Well, tone down that groaning because help has arrived. It comes straight from students who have battled the homework monster—and won!

In this book, 300 top high school juniors and seniors from around the country share their secrets for surviving homework. They aren't wild about homework. They grumble about it, too. But over the years, they've found ways to handle the homework hassle. In fact, they've handled it so well, most wound up on their high school's honor roll.

These savvy high school juniors and seniors described their study secrets by filling out a special four-page "Surviving Homework" questionnaire. It asked how they dealt with the major homework gripes younger kids have. The list of gripes came from a poll of 100 fourth through eighth graders, as well as from other recent homework surveys.

The high school juniors and seniors who filled out the "Surviving Homework" questionnaires jotted down all kinds of super study ideas. This book presents many of them.

Some of their study tips are a bit unusual. That's okay, say the experts. Researchers have found that there's no one best way to study. People learn in many different ways. The key to success is to have a set of strategies that work for you. So check out the tips in this book to see which ones to add to your bag of tricks, to help make homework less of a hassle for you.

GRIPE #1
THE "IT'S S-O-O-O-O BORING" BLUES

What a bore! If you feel that way about homework, join the crowd! A hundred fourth to eighth graders were asked what bugs them about homework. Nearly all griped that some assignments are s-o-o-o-o boring.

So did many of the 300 high school juniors and seniors whose study tips are featured in this book. Did these high schoolers find ways to beat the homework blahs? You bet! Read on to see how.

GOOF OFF

How can you goof off and do homework at the same time? "If the assignment was to put twenty spelling words in sentences, I'd make up goofy sentences," said Heather, one of the high school students who shared their tricks for how to slog through boring homework. But she warned, "Make sure the words are used correctly—just put them in a ridiculous situation."

Many of the teens had fun goofing off with their spelling sentences. Tim liked making his "morbid" or scary. Some turned theirs into tongue twisters or picked a theme for the sentences, such as "What I Want for My Birthday." Others had their sentences describe a movie, report on a news or sports event, or even tell a joke.

GET SNAZZY

"Instead of concentrating on how boring an assignment was, I'd work on fancy handwriting while writing the answers," said Juliet. Writing in different colors might also snazz up a dreary worksheet. But if you have to hand in that worksheet, make sure your teacher would go for the colorful look.

10

GIMME A BREAK!

"Take breaks," said Charles. Many of our high school advisers battled the blahs that way. They'd do a few dull problems until they started going bonkers. Then they'd tackle something else. It could be something fun—shooting a few hoops or dancing to a funky beat. Or it could be a different assignment. After a while, they'd switch back to old dreary-o again. "If you do a few problems at a time, it seems less boring," said Reagan.

Taking breaks can help even if the homework isn't dull. Your brain gets sluggish if you sit glued to your books for too long. Some experts say to take a five-minute study break every thirty minutes or so. Tia liked to *start* her homework with a break. She'd do something active before studying, like roller blading, to get her energy up. She found that studying zipped along much faster if she did something fun first.

AND THE WINNER IS ...

Some of our homework whizzes didn't just take a break. They gave themselves a *prize* during the break. But to get the prize, they had to finish a big chunk of work first. Here are some of the treats they used as prizes: having a snack, phoning a friend, listening to music, taking a walk, reading an exciting book, watching TV, or lifting weights.

SPEED DEMONS

"Trying to get a dull assignment done in a certain time limit made it more challenging and fun," said Carolyn. She'd set a time limit for a whole assignment and try to beat it. Others would time each problem to see if they could do each new one faster than the one before. Just be careful you don't zoom along so fast you smash up by getting the answers wrong.

ADD MUSIC

"For homework that was boring and didn't require a lot of thought, I'd listen to music," said Luke. So did many of the other teens. Some flipped on music to get pumped up and ready for work. Others used music to relax or because the rhythm kept them working at a steady pace.

But musical studying won't work for everyone. Experts have found that while many people actually do better if they study to a little background music, others need peace and quiet to concentrate. Some people, like Brian, can mix music with only certain subjects. Music would help him zip through math, but he said, "I can't read to music."

What music did these teens use for studying? All kinds—from rock to classical to pop to jazz. Many preferred music with no singing so

they didn't get distracted by the words. But there was one thing most of these successful students almost NEVER flipped on while studying—the TV. It's tough to keep your eyes on your books with all those images flickering away on the tube.

IMAGINE THAT!

Several of our homework aces beat the blahs by letting their imaginations run wild. "With math homework, I'd pretend I was an accountant 'working' for people to figure out how much money they had," said Jennifer. Or she'd pretend a dull foreign language drill was a secret code she had to crack.

BUDDY UP

"I'd do boring assignments with friends," said Paul. "Our personalities would make the homework less boring." Having a friend scribbling away nearby can help ease the pain of working your way through a blah worksheet. But some teens turned thumbs down to studying with friends—too much joking around to get anything done. Others found ways to keep the joking under control. They'd set aside the first few minutes for fun and then get down to business. If things started getting out of hand, they'd either call it quits or someone would remind everybody to hush up and hit the books.

SPEAK UP

Some teens took drastic action. They grew so fed up with dull worksheets that they got up their courage and—*gasp*—told the teacher. Surprise! That strategy often worked! Siromani told what happened after she and her friends spoke up: "We were doing monotonous activities in history. Then we spoke up. Our teacher compromised and gave us some assignments that were different and more fun." Another brave student even got his teacher to admit that his worksheets were boring to grade, too. Result? That teacher found more lively ways to design his assignments.

Of course, some students struck out when they spoke up. Either their teachers were set in their ways, or drill work turned out to be the best way to practice the material. Kelsey felt the secret to success lay in *how* you spoke up. "If you tell teachers in a positive and constructive manner that you'd like them to spice things up, they're generally agreeable," she said. "They want to help you learn, not make you die of boredom."

OVER AND OUT

Instead of searching for ways to make a dull assignment less boring, Meredith used a different approach. "I'd just sit down and do it," she said. "Often I'd use up more time complaining than it would take to just get it over with."

Believe it or not, some teens actually *liked* drab and dreary drills. "They're a nice break from more intense homework," said Sarah. She also found that doing the same type of math problem over and over "helped it become second nature to me." Laura noted that "hearing a teacher gab can get you only so far. You need hands-on practice to absorb the information."

GRIPE #2
THE TIME CRUNCH

Finding time to *do* homework is another big headache—a very familiar one for our high school advisers. They were super busy with activities and clubs, but most still managed to squeeze in two hours or more of homework a day. Here's how they fit in the fun stuff—and homework, too.

BATTLE PLAN

"I made lists of things I had to do," said Laura. "That way what little extra time I had could be spent wisely." She must have put her list on very *long* paper because during her senior year she was into so many activities: swimming, theater, band, orchestra, choir, the German Club, 4-H, color guard, and a youth group. *(Whew!)* But when she looked at her list, she could still find time to fit in studying. "Everything can get done," she said. "It's a matter of budgeting time."

Like Laura, most of our advisers made a battle plan—a master schedule of how to squeeze in all their activities, their homework, *and* some free time (important, too!).

Many wrote out their schedules in small diary-type notebooks they carried around all day. Some notebooks had a separate page for each week—others had a separate page for each day. These books came in handy for jotting down each night's assignment as teachers announced them. Some teens also logged in their schedules on big wall calendars at home.

How to write up a schedule? One way is to start as Laura did—by writing down on whatever calendar you use all the activities you know are coming up. If you have soccer practice on Mondays from 5:00 to 6:00 P.M., write that on every Monday. Then take a look at the time that's left each day. Figure out a good place to stick an hour or two of solid study time. Jodi found that setting aside the same block of time each day for homework made it easier to get into the studying habit.

"I'd circle days on my calendar when I didn't have to go to work or to a meeting," said Rachel. "I tried to spend those whole afternoons on homework, working ahead." That kept her from getting in a jam on days when she was more booked up. Others used weekends to catch up or get ahead.

Many students didn't seem to mind having jam-packed schedules. In fact, several felt that being in tons of activities actually made it easier to knuckle down and get homework done. As Toya said: "It taught me how to organize my time."

THE BIG SQUEEZE

To fit all their homework into their schedules, many of our super-busy advisers had to track down every spare moment. Here's how:

- **Un-*home*-work.** "Try to finish as much as you can *in school*," said Jennifer. Charay agreed: "I'd do homework at lunch, during homeroom, or even when there was extra time if I finished a test early. Whenever I'd get a chance in school, I'd do some math problems or read something for English."

- **Break time.** "I'd squeeze homework in *between* after-school activities," said Ben. That's when many teens knocked off busy-work assignments—ones that didn't require too much concentration. They'd zip through a worksheet while being driven to piano lessons, or review vocabulary flash cards during breaks in basketball practice.

- **Rise 'n shine.** "I'd get up early to do homework in the morning while my mind was fresh," said Rocky. Early risers often found it easier to study at the crack of dawn. It was quieter then, and they didn't get interrupted by phoning friends.

READY - SET - GO

What about those days when there's so much homework, you don't know *where* to start? Our tip-givers used different strategies to pick which assignment to tackle first. Some would start with the assignment

20

that had the highest "priority." (That means it was most important or due first.) Then, they'd do the rest of the subjects in the order in which they'd have them in school the next day. That way if they didn't finish the work for the last subject, they might still have time to do it at lunch the next day before having that subject.

Others would whiz through the *easiest* work first. "The more you finish, the more confident you feel, which makes it easier to continue," said Heather. But some did exactly the opposite and plunged into the *hardest* work first, when they felt most alert. A few used yet another approach—getting all the boring stuff out of the way first so they'd want to keep going to get to the fun stuff. No matter which strategy they used, taking breaks made a heavy load seem less overwhelming.

HUNTING TIME

Some students looked at their schedules and—*eek!*—found they didn't have enough time for everything. How did they free up more study time?

- **Hang up.** "Cutting back the time I spent on the phone helped a lot," said Cari.

- **Tune out.** "Cut down on TV watching," said Luke. "That can free up a lot of time."

- **Drop it.** Others made a tough choice and dropped one of their many activities. Did they feel bummed out? Sure, but also relieved. One girl reported feeling "less stressed" after quitting her after-school job. When Matt dropped one of his sports—wrestling—he found "it was easier to get my homework done."

GRIPE #3
MEMORIZING MADNESS

The secret to memorizing is to force your brain to pay close attention while you load a fact into your memory bank. If your brain notices a fact going *in*, it's more likely to be able to yank it *out* when test time rolls around. Our teen advisers used lots of tricks to grab the attention of their brains—from singing to scribbling to springing about. People learn in different ways. Some do best by seeing things, others by hearing them, while others need to be active to learn. Check out our advisers' tricks. Which fit your learning style?

GET SILLY

"I made up sentences with the first letter of each word I had to memorize," said Emily. So did many students. Some of their sentences were pretty silly. Here's one that helped Paul: "**K**ings **P**lay **C**hess **O**n **F**at **G**uys' **S**tomachs **S**ometimes." It got him to remember this list of terms for classifying animals: **K**ingdom, **P**hylum, **C**lass, **O**rder, **F**amily, **G**enus, **S**pecies, **S**ubspecies.

Or how about this one: "**M**y **V**ery **E**legant **M**other **J**ust **S**at **U**pon **N**ine **P**ins." It helps in remembering the planets and their order in the solar system: **M**ercury, **V**enus, **E**arth, **M**ars, **J**upiter, **S**aturn, **U**ranus, **N**epture, **P**luto.

Instead of a sentence, other teens used a word, such as **HOMES** (to remember the names of the five Great Lakes). Erika made up **LABB** to remember that **L**incoln was **A**ssassinated **B**y **B**ooth.

Larissa fooled around with the *sounds* in words. She remembered that "anarchy" meant "rebelling" by creating this sentence: "Ants aren't going." The "an" sound in "anarchy" reminded her of her rebellious ants, which helped her think of the definition.

The sillier you get, the better your brain will remember, said several of our master memorizers. Silly memory tricks like these have a fancy name—*mnemonics*. Hmm, what goofy sentence can help you remember how to spell that?

RHYME TIME

Rhymes made memorizing a snap for many teens. That's how Rachel remembered the amendments to the Constitution. For example, with amendment number four, she thought: "Four—door." That reminded her that to get in someone's door, police need a search warrant, which is what the Fourth Amendment is all about.

LINK IT

"Hook the facts to something in your life," said Rosten. Many students did that to remember historical dates. They linked the dates to family members' ages, friends' birth dates, phone numbers, or historical dates they already knew. For example, people born in 1978 could easily remember the date of the Louisiana Purchase (1803) once they realized it was 175 years before their birth. The year Jefferson died (1826) would be a snap to recall if you realized it was 50 years after a date nearly everyone knows—1776.

Many teens also mastered vocabulary words by linking them to something familiar. One girl never forgot the meaning of "insolent" (insulting) after thinking to herself: "My brother is insolent."

OUTSTANDING!

Another memorizing trick: Make an item to be memorized stand out from the crowd, so it is special in some way. Melissa used that trick to master French vocabulary. For example, she made one French phrase seem special by making a big deal of one of its letters. The phrase was "avoir **r**aison," which means "to be right." She noticed that "**r**aison" and "**r**ight" both start with "**r**." From then on, whenever she saw "avoir **r**aison," she'd think of the letter "**r**," which led her to the "**r**ight" meaning.

Heather made two spelling demons stand out in her mind by making up a little rule about them. The spelling demons were:

- "de<u>s</u>ert" (a sandy place), which has *one* "s"

- "de<u>ss</u>ert" (the food), which has *two* "s's."

Her rule: "When having de<u>ss</u>ert, you always want *two*, but you want to be lost in a de<u>s</u>ert only *once.* "

PICTURE, PLEASE

Jonathan made items more memorable by imagining pictures of them. "Picture an object and make it do a silly action with what you have to remember," he said. "To remember that an ant can carry ten times its body weight, I'd visualize an ant carrying a huge number 10 on its back."

SOUND OFF!

Musical memorizing was a hit with many teens. Brad would set facts he had to learn to old, familiar tunes. To nail down some geography facts, he sang, "Someone's in the kitchen with Dinah, Vietnam is right below China." Our musical memorizers crooned their homework to all kinds of songs, from "I've Been Working on the Railroad" to more rousing rock and rap numbers. "It's easier to remember things that have a rhythm to them," said Erika.

Other teens sounded off in a different way. Instead of singing, they'd say out loud things they had to memorize. "I'd talk to myself and explain the information to myself," said Christine. Or they'd record it on a tape that they'd listen to again and again. As John noted: "That helped me learn the information in two ways—by saying it and hearing it."

SHOW OFF

"To memorize vocabulary words, I'd try to use them while talking to people," said Charay. "By using the words in context, I'd understand them better. If you do this with friends from class, it can be fun, almost like a joke." Laura agreed. She liked to surprise friends by using biology terms in conversation, such as: "Take your phalanges out of your orifice." (One possible rough translation: "Take your fingers out of your mouth.")

SCRIBBLE, SCRITCH

"I'm a visual learner," said Liz. "If I write down words or dates a few times, I can memorize them much more easily." That write-on strategy helped many students. Some would just write the word or phrase over and over, or they'd write up pretend matching tests for themselves to take.

27

But others found more unusual ways to practice writing what they had to memorize. "I'd write the word so it looked like what it means," said Peggy. Other ways to add zing to practicing vocabulary or spelling words: Snake the words along in a curvy, wiggly line, or arrange them to make a fantastic design.

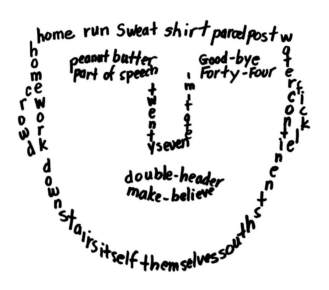

FLASH!

Another way to practice writing things that have to be memorized: Make flash cards. "I'd put the word on one side of an index card and the definition on the other," said Michele. Then she'd drill herself. After mastering a word, she'd take its card out of her stack.

Ryan liked using notecards because they were so easy to carry. He'd write down facts he had to learn on notecards and carry them around with him wherever he went. When he had a spare moment, he'd whip out his cards for a quick look-through. Other teens used flash cards to play games, such as Memory. In a game like that, one card in a pair to be matched could be a vocabulary word, and the other card could be the meaning.

28

So as not to spend a fortune on notecards, Michele suggested a way to make a pack of cards go farther: Cut them in half (or fourths) before using them.

STICK 'EM UP

"I stuck little notes with a word and its definition by every light switch at home," said Jacob. "When I turned on a light, I'd read the note." Lester stuck stuff up, too—*way* up. He wrote his German vocabulary words in huge letters and taped them to his ceiling so he could lie down and study.

MOVE IT!

"I move around when I have to memorize things," said Elizabeth. "I don't know why, but it helps." Educators have found that moving around lets some students focus their minds better on what they're studying so they can learn it more easily. "I jump around or pace and chant stuff to myself I absolutely need to know," said Carlos. Some teens even take vocabulary lists along while jogging. As Todd noted: "Moving around gives you energy and enthusiasm." Yolanda noted another moving-around advantage: "When I'm getting tired, it helps me wake up."

WHOA!

Don't try to cram a long list of items into your brain all at once. Many of our study whizzes found that memorizing went easier if they split a list into chunks and worked on only a few items at a time. Jonathan added a fun twist to this. With spelling words, he'd learn all the words that contained a certain letter, such as "t." After taking a break, he'd see how many of those "t" words he still remembered. Next, he'd tackle all the words with another letter, and so on.

GRIPE #4
WRITER'S BLOCK

STOP! If your story is stalled at the starting gate, don't waste gobs of time staring at that blank sheet of paper. Sneak a peek at our high school advisers' surprising suggestions.

FORGET IT

That's right! Many writer's-block sufferers said to forget about a writing assignment—at least for a while.

When Kevin found himself stumped for a story idea, he'd "stop and do something else. Then, an idea would usually pop right into my head."

Students would do all kinds of things to take the pressure off their story-stumped brains. They'd shoot hoops, take a walk, listen to music, cook, or even have a bath. While they were keeping busy, that story assignment would still be bubbling away somewhere in the back of their brains. Before long, a story idea would burst out, when least expected.

SEARCH PARTY

Some frustrated writers would go searching for inspiration. "I'd flip through an encyclopedia for story ideas," said Chris. Others would look through magazines or newspapers for pictures that might spark an idea. Michael would "draw a shape and create something out of it to write about."

Peggy made a game out of the search for a story idea. "Open a dictionary, close your eyes and pick a word," she said. "Think of all the things you could write about related to that word. Or spin the globe, pick a place and set a story there."

Still stumped? Round up some helpers for your search party. "Ask parents for ideas," said Sarah.

ZOOM IN ON YOU

"Draw on your own life," said Lissett. "Think of personal experiences that relate to the topic. People write best if they write from experience." What if you feel nothing interesting ever happens to you? Start with a real event and "stretch the truth to make it exciting," said Juliet. Or write about something you *wish* would happen.

Corinne's tip: "Use your friends, change their names, and have something funny happen." For example, imagine how some of your friends would react if they turned a corner and ran smack into something truly unusual. A Komodo dragon, perhaps? Or a prehistoric cave dweller. Or a famous sports star.

What if the teacher assigned the story topics and you got one that leaves you cold? Many of our tip-givers would still try to work in their favorite subjects. Say the topic is space travel (which you hate) but you love animals. Write about an astronaut taking a pet dog on a shuttle flight. Or make the astronaut a frog!

BRAINSTORM

"Write down a list of all the ideas and topics you can think of," said Alisa. Add anything that pops into your mind, even if it seems stupid. "You might change your mind later or find a way to make that idea work," said Michele. Some students jotted down ideas helter-skelter. "Circle things. Draw arrows from one word to another. Go crazy," said Carlos. Others wrote their ideas under headings, such as: Characters, Places, Plots.

After filling a page with tons of ideas, they'd pick a few for the assignment. What about all the other ideas? Some students added them to a list of possible story ideas they stashed in their notebooks. That list would come in handy next time writer's block struck.

SKIP AROUND

Often the hardest part of writing a story is getting the first sentence down on paper. So skip it, advised George. "I'd start a story in the middle," he said. He'd come up with a good opener later, after he felt more at ease with his topic. Juliet found another way to skip *writing* that first sentence—she'd talk it out first. "I'd talk to myself about the ideas I had. It's easier to write a sentence after forming it verbally," she said. Or talk about your topic into a tape recorder. Listening to the tape can help you find a way to start writing.

SUPER STORY-STARTERS

- "Start with a startling statistic or eye-catching quote," said Alisha.

- "Start with a question because it leads you through the topic as you try to explain the answer," said Edie. Or begin by writing: "What if ..."

- "Start like a fairy tale," said Sarah.

- "Use time twists, going forward or backward in time," said Leah.

- "Start with a joke—*if* it applies to the subject," said Laura.

- "Write what an animal might be thinking," said Corinne.

I WONDER IF IT'S TRUE THAT PEOPLE HAVE NINE LIVES ...

GRIPE # 5
BOOK REPORT PAIN

Our teen advisers' number-one remedy for book report pain: If given a choice, pick a book that interests you. That's bound to make the report more fun. But even if you're stuck with a dud of a book, the report doesn't have to be a dud. Over the years, our savvy high schoolers jazzed up book reports with all kinds of offbeat approaches. Take a look at their lineup of great pain relievers.

SOME OFFBEAT APPROACHES THAT MADE DOING BOOK REPORTS LESS OF A PAIN:

"I did the book report as if it were the journal of one of the characters. I browned the paper and bound it with leather straps so it looked like an old journal," said Danielle.

"I pretended I was the author and wrote a new ending for the book, what I thought would happen if the author had kept going," said Alisa.

WELL, I'LL TELL **YOU**, WHEN CAPTAIN AHAB SPIED OLD MOBY AGAIN THAT MORNING...

"I wrote the report as if I were a newscaster doing a news story on the events in the book. With friends, I also did a video on the report, just like a news show," said Reagan.

"I used my computer and added graphics to the report," said Kevin.

"I pretended I was a spy on a secret mission reporting on the book to my commanding officer," said Melissa.

"I did a book report from an alien's point of view," said Tia.

"Put humor in it," said Ben.

OH... STOP... **STOP!** MY BINDING IS SPLITTING!

"I made a cassette tape of me doing a pretend interview with the author. I played both parts," said Elisabeth.

"Tell the story from the point of view of one of the characters," said Roger.

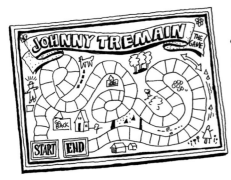

"I made a board game based on the book," said Amanda.

"Pretend you're selling the book. Write a rave review," said Juliet.

"I did a CD-ROM video presentation on one book," said David.

"I baked a cake and put the title of the book—*The Secret Garden*—on the cake. I made a garden on the cake with frosting and used little people figures for the characters. I wrote a summary of the book and read it to the class. After I read it, we all enjoyed the cake. It was fun." said Corinne.

WARNING

For a *very* offbeat idea, run it by your teacher before you start, just to be sure it's okay.

P.S. "It's easier if you finish reading the book *before* doing the report," said Mike.

GRIPE #6
SPACING OUT

After spacing out (or snoozing out) again and again, our high school advisers came up with ways to prevent an attack of textbook-reading M.E.G.O. (That stands for My Eyes Glaze Over.) Maybe their tips can help you head off the z-z-z-z-z's next time you have to—yawn—wade through a thick, murky textbook chapter.

SNOOZE PATROL

Here are a few basic tricks our tip-givers used to stay wide awake while reading:

- **Don't get too comfy.** Many followed Kally's strategy: "I sit up straight when reading so as not to fall asleep." Others recommended turning the lights up bright. Edie warned: "Don't lie down to read." If you get too snuggly, you may soon be snoozing.

- **Break it up.** "If you start to space out, stop reading for a while," said Todd. Erika agreed: "I don't read a whole assignment at once. I break it into sections and read a section at a time."

- **Splash.** When getting sleepy, many teens used the water treatment. They'd take a sip of cold water or splash it on their faces. One girl found that tooth-brushing would wake her up enough to finish a rough reading assignment.

- **Shhhh.** Many students found music and reading didn't mix. They turned their music *off* while reading, even though they liked it *on* for drill-type homework. Liz offered another bit of advice: "Sit away from the TV."

- **Start early.** "Don't read late at night," said Mike. Read earlier when you're not so drowsy.

CHECK IT OUT

Another trick many students used: Check out a chapter *before* reading it. "I'd look at the headings and words in italics first," said Melissa. Others would start by glancing at the pictures in the chapter and reading the captions. Or they'd look over the review questions or summary at the end of a chapter.

All this chapter-checking gave them an idea of what the chapter would be about. It's like looking at a roadmap before heading out on a trip.

The checking could also help possible snoozers think up questions to answer as they read. Looking for answers could help keep their minds from wandering. Students could either use the chapter's review questions or make up their own from the chapter's headings. For example, if one heading was "Causes of the War of 1812," that could be turned into a question: "What were the causes of the War?" While reading, a student could look for the answer. As Kami noted: "Be thinking while you read."

Once Peggy started reading, she'd stop now and then to summarize what she'd read or to answer the questions she had in mind. If she reached the end of a section and pulled a blank as to what the section was about, no problem. She'd just read that section again.

Educators have given strategies like these fancy names, such as "**SQ3R**." That stands for:

Survey a chapter to think up ...

Questions, and then ...

Read for the answers, and then ...

Recite the answers, and finally ...

Review.

The basic point of SQ3R and other similar methods is just what our teens found: Reading goes more smoothly if you check it out first.

JOT IT DOWN

"I don't just read," said Lissett. "I *do* something like highlight important facts (if I own the book) or take notes." That helps in staying alert and remembering what you read. Well-written notes also make studying for tests a lot easier.

How do you take notes without copying over the *whole* chapter? "First, I'd read it, and then go back and take notes ," said Vonetta. By the end of the chapter, she'd know what was important in it. She could take notes just on that. Charay used this strategy, too. But during her first read-through, she'd jot down unfamiliar words to look up later.

There are many ways to take notes. Here are a few our expert note takers used:

- "I'd write my notes in an informal outline," said Lynn. "I'd start by copying down the heading of each section in the chapter. Then I'd list the key ideas of that passage under the heading."

- "I'd write a short one-sentence summary of each paragraph," said Rachel.

- "I'd pick out the main idea from each section," said Todd. "Then I'd paraphrase it (write it in my own words)."

45

TO MAKE NOTES EASIER TO USE . . .

- Put information on different topics in different colors. A big help, according to Danielle.
- Add diagrams. That made it easier for Reagan to remember how things worked.
- To keep from losing notes, Peggy kept all her notes (and assignments) for each subject in a separate folder. Using separate sections in a notebook would work just as well.

In addition to these notes, many students also kept lists of important words, dates, places, and people that were mentioned in the chapter. "I'd write down all the words in **boldface** or *italics*, and their meanings," said Tim.

"Write your notes the way you talk," Christine said. Pretend to explain the information to a friend. "You don't have to use complete sentences," said Anissa. But include enough detail so you'll remember the point of the passage.

JABBER, JABBER

Lynn's secret to staying awake while reading: "I'd read out loud to keep my mind from wandering." Too shy to try? "If you study in your room, no one can hear you," said Peggy, "so who cares?" Some teens even used funny voices and accents while they read aloud.

Carolyn found another way talking could help. Right after reading a chapter, she'd discuss it with a parent or friend. That helped her remember it better.

MAKE A MOVIE

Make the movie in your *head,* of course. That's what Jennifer did. "I'd visualize in my mind what I'd read, so the material became the script of a movie," she said. Several teens used this approach. "I'd try to picture real people dealing with the problems, inventions, or other things described," said Kathy.

Others found different ways to let their imaginations liven up reading. Tia said to pretend you're a scientist, poet, or historian, and the information in the chapter is important to your work. Toya's strategy: "I think of reading as being able to travel for free, a way to go to places and see things you've never seen before. If you think of reading that way, it's easier to remember what you read."

GRIPE #7
PROJECT PANIC

A few of the teens who revealed their study habits for this book admitted that they, too, left projects to the last minute. A very few even claimed to *like* working under time pressure. But most of these top students did not. They found other ways to handle projects so they didn't get into a last-minute tizzy. Give your nerves a rest and give their tips a try.

MINI-MIZE IT

Don't think of a project as one great big, humongous assignment. That kind of thinking is bound to freeze you up so you'll never start. Instead, try Christine's strategy. "I'd break up a project into little mini-projects," she said. "I'd do one mini-project at a time." That can make the assignment seem less overwhelming. For example, if you had to do a report on United States rivers, you could give yourself a set of smaller assignments, such as: Read About Rivers in the East, Read About Rivers in the West, Draw a Map, Design a Cover, etc. As Ami noted:

"If you do a lot of little tasks, it seems like you're hardly doing anything."

TIMELINE

"I'd write out a timeline for myself," said Michele. "I'd plan to have so much done by such a day, more done by another day, and so on. I'd plan to finish a few days before the project was due so I'd have time to deal with unforeseen problems." No last-minute panic for her.

With projects where she had to pick the topic, her first deadline would be to get that topic picked. Smart move. Some kids spend so long searching for the "perfect topic" they run out of time. "Any topic can be exciting if you take the right approach," said Rusty.

Charles recommended getting going on a project "as soon as possible. I'd hit the library and start researching the first weekend. Most projects can be finished quickly if you work on them a little each night."

Timeline for My Project on Carnivorous Plants

PROJECT DUE: MONDAY, THE 31st !!

| SAT (15th) Go to Library. Get books on carnivorous plants. | MON-WED (17th-19th) Read about the plants. Take notes. | THURS (20th) Draw pictures of some plants and their victims. | FRI (21st) Call Mom's friend, Drake Q. Lahh... See if we can visit on Sat. to see his carnivorous plants. | SAT (22nd) Visit Mr. Lahh with Mom. Interview him & observe plants. Take notes & make drawings. |

STRANGE BUT TRUE

What if the teacher handed out topics for projects and the one you got is the pits? "I'd try to find things that would make that dull topic unusual—or maybe even *strange*," said Charles. For a project on fish, you could search for information on weird fish, such as the anglerfish (which uses "bait" to catch other fish). You could present all the basic fishy facts your report had to include while describing the oddballs you uncovered.

SMILE!

Brian's remedy for a dull project: "Make it humorous." A report on the digestive system—*ugh*—could become an accident-prone water-slide ride down the throat—*whoosh*—into the stomach—*splurp*—through the intestines, and so forth. Or make the report like an episode of a TV show. Yolanda's tip: "Look at the information in an unusual way. Explain the funny things that might happen if you didn't mix the right elements in the right way for a physics experiment." Some teachers might not go for the light touch, but many would. After all, they get bored, too.

SUN (23rd)	MON-WED (24th-26th)	THU-FRI (27th-28th)	SAT (29th)	SUN (30th)	MON (31st)
Make clay model of one of plants.	Write rough draft of report.	Fix up report. Do final draft.	Draw cover for report.	Put report together.	Hand in report and clay model.

PROJECT PERK-ER-UPPERS

- **Make a video.** "I made a video on mollusks for biology with some friends," said Chad. "Not only did the video contain all the necessary information, but we had fun. The outcome was hilarious."

- **Write a poem.** "Instead of writing a report, write a poem. I once did a factual report as a poem," said David.

- **Build a model.** "Building things makes a project fun," said Kally. "For a report on the Sistine Chapel, I made a model of it."

- **Grow something.** "For a report on ferns, I built a terrarium to go with it," said Rusty. "It was neat to watch the ferns grow."

- **Serve food.** "A group of friends and I did a project on Czechoslovakia," said Alisa. "We made a Czech dessert for the class."

- **Add music.** "Once I played live music at the end of a report, which won bonus points," said Patrick.

DIG DEEPER

When faced with a less-than-thrilling project, Peggy would see if she could st-r-e-t-c-h the assignment so it would connect with something that interested her. For a report on Shakespeare, she found a way to make it include something she really liked—movies. She took one of Shakespeare's plays, *Romeo and Juliet*, and showed how its basic theme kept turning up in movies. "I made a video and included clips from movies, such as *Gone With the Wind*," she explained.

If all else failed, Tyde had one last trick up his sleeve. He'd take a deep breath and ask the teacher *(in private)* if he could switch to another topic.

CARD TRICKS

After settling on a topic and a schedule, it's time to plunge into the tough jobs of researching and writing up the report. Our tip-givers found a way to make that less of a grind. They did some tricks with cards—notecards, that is.

- **One-FACT-per-card trick.** While doing reading for a report, students would bring along a pack of notecards. Some would write just *one fact* on each card. After finishing the research, they'd sort their cards. They'd put all those on a certain subject together.

53

"When it was time to write the report, I'd arrange the cards in the order of what I'd want to discuss," said Jennifer. Then she'd write by working her way through her stack of cards. "You can flip through the cards, discard ones you don't want to use, and reorganize things so easily," said Sarah.

- **One-TOPIC-per-card trick.** Other students used their cards differently. They'd write each subject to be covered in the report at the top of a card. For a report on blood, one card might be labeled "Red Cells." Then every fact learned about red blood cells would go on that card. Facts on white blood cells would go on a card called "White Cells," and so on. At writing time, the student would decide in which order to cover the subjects, put the cards in order, and write.

Tim used this same basic method, but didn't use cards. He used sheets of paper labeled for the different subjects.

MORE NOTES ON NOTES

- "Have an outline in mind of what you want to include in the report *before* taking notes," said Benjamin. That way you won't waste time taking notes on stuff you don't really need.

- "Keep your notes simple and to the point," said Andrew. Put quotation marks around things you copy word-for-word. Then when you write the report, you can decide to use a direct quote or to summarize the quote in your own words. Be sure to jot down the book and page number where you found the information.

- "Do bibliography cards, too," advised Jennifer. Those are cards that list each book you read, giving its title, author, publisher, etc. Then when you're about to hand in your report, you don't have to *panic* when you suddenly remember you need a bibliography. Just whip out your bibliography cards, instead of dashing around to find all the books you used.

- "I'd make a photocopy of an article," said Matthew. "Then I'd highlight information I needed right on the copy."

- "Write neatly so you can use your notes later," warned Juliet.

GRIPE #8
OOPS! WRONG STUFF

Our high school advisers knew all about getting in a muddle like that. One boy claimed to be an expert at finding oodles of ways to NOT to start homework. "I've got it down to a science," he said, "throwing paper wads at the trash can, sharpening a pencil over and over." But others found ways to "Oops!"-proof their studying.

THE WRITE STUFF

To keep from bringing home the wrong stuff, Luke said: "Write down all your assignments *as soon as* they're given." He and many others did that in a handy little notebook they toted around all day.

Then comes the *hard* part. As Kristina explained: "You have to LOOK at the assignment book every day *before* leaving school to see what books to bring home." How to remember? Some teens tied a string around a finger. Seeing the string reminded

NOW IF I COULD JUST REMEMBER WHAT THIS STRING **MEANS**...

them to check the assignment book. Others wrote reminders on their hands. After a while, most got in the habit of checking that little life-saving book. What if they forgot and came home without the foggiest idea of what the math homework was? Relief was just a phone call away. They'd call up a friend who was in their class.

PACK IT UP

Another goof-proof tip: Use your book bag as a traveling file cabinet. "I'd put all the important stuff I needed right in my book bag," said Stephen. After math class if you know you'll need your math book that night, stuff it in your pack. Then to keep from forgetting to bring stuff back to school from home, Luke advised: "When you finish an assignment at home, put it right back in your book bag."

THE ROUND UP

"Have all your school supplies together and put them in a place at home where they'll be easy to find," said Chris. That can help you avoid that great time waster—the nightly hunt for a pencil, pen, and something to write on. Our tip-givers stashed their school supplies in different spots: in a basket stored in a hall closet, in a desk drawer, in a box on a bookshelf. Many kept extra pencils, pens, and paper in their book bags so they'd always be ready for action.

THE PERFECT SPOT

Another key to getting rolling on homework is to have a nice, quiet place to do it. For one high school senior, that's "any place where no one will bug me." But many teens had a special spot at home where they did most of their homework. It was fairly distraction free, although some teens often had to ask family members in the next room to—*puh-l-e-a-s-e*—turn down the volume on the TV.

58

Many students studied in their own rooms, but not Kelsey. "I can't study in my room," she said. "I get sidetracked with my radio and other stuff. So I study at the kitchen table." Others studied in their living or dining rooms. Some switched around—doing math at their desks and reading in the living room. One girl claimed to do her best studying in the bathroom, where she could definitely get peace and quiet. But for Roger, sometimes no place at home would do. So he'd "get out of the house and go to a place without any distractions, like the library."

ON CALL

Okay, you finally knuckle down to work. "Rrringg!" There's a phone call for you. Should you take it? "Sure," said Loretta. "Sometimes the break will do you good." But Jamie added: "I wouldn't talk too long because I'd begin to lose my train of thought on the homework I was doing." Others said if they were in the middle of something complicated, they'd tell the person they'd call back later.

GRIPE #9
IN A FOG

Turning the paper upside down probably won't help. Nor will shaking it, twisting it, or folding it into an origami giraffe. For fog-clearing strategies that really do help, read on.

STOP!

"When I got confused with an assignment, I'd get away from it for about ten minutes," said Megan. She'd take a break or work on another subject for a while. "Then I'd begin again with a clear mind." Often that was enough to blow away the fog.

If the puzzler was a math problem, instead of putting the *whole* assignment aside, some teens would just skip the tricky problem and go on to other problems in the same assignment. They might be worded differently, and that might help in figuring out how to solve the troublemaker.

SLOW DOWN

"Go slow!" That's Alisa's advice for how to handle a tricky assignment. "Read it over and over until you get the hang of it."

Our teen advisers found that strategy especially helpful with math word problems. "I'd always read a word problem once without writing anything down," said Liz. She'd concentrate on trying to understand what the problem was all about. Rusty would ask himself questions as he read: "What does the problem want? What does it give me?" He'd keep a lookout for key words, such as: "is" (which usually means equals). The next step would be to go back and read through the problem again, writing down *everything*. Laura would use two headings:

- **"Givens"** - the facts the problem gives;
- **"Find"** - what it asks you to find out.

That approach should help you figure out what to do. If not, check out the next tip—The Big Clue.

THE BIG CLUE

"The method to use in solving a homework problem is 99% of the time the one you learned in class that day," said Larissa. So drag out the notes you took on the problems you worked in class. If you didn't take any notes in class, you're out of luck. Make a note to always copy down the example problem the teacher gives in class. Justin added: "Try to practice it right after it's explained so you'll remember it later." If you get fouled up, ask the teacher to run through the problem again.

After getting home, several students said they'd zip through the sample problem from class one more time before tackling that night's homework. That way they'd have the right method clearly in mind before their brains had a chance to get foggy.

QUICK PIX

"I'd always draw a picture of what a math word problem was saying," said Kally. "I'm a very visual person and this helped me understand what the question was asking." Drawing pictures or diagrams helped many of the teens not only with math, but with science and other subjects as well. Carlos drew a diagram to figure out who did what to whom in that super-complicated play by Shakespeare, *Macbeth*.

Heather suggested using different colored pens or pencils in your

1. Who has the most baseball cards?
   Bob has more than Fido but less than Mike.
   Becky has more than Mike.
   Chad has more than Mike, but can't beat Becky.

BECKY   CHAD   MIKE   BOB   FIDO

WHAT'S A "BASEBALL CARD?"

diagrams. That makes it easier to see connections among the different pieces of information.

OPEN YOUR MOUTH

If all else fails, there's another way out of the fog: Ask for help! "I'd call my smartest friend," said Andrew. "Or I'd ask my parents. Or I'd ask the teacher the next day."

One way to get help from the teacher: Simply ask a question in class. "Don't be afraid to do that," said Stacey. "You're probably not the only one in class with that question." Others preferred to get their help from the teacher one-on-one, either by going in before school or hanging around afterward. The teacher may be able to get you back on the right track, or may set up some special tutoring sessions that will help clear up your confusion. Going to the teacher can pay off in yet another way. As Matthew noted: "It shows you're putting in extra effort." Teachers like that.

STRENGTH IN NUMBERS

Instead of waiting to call a friend only when total confusion struck, many teens organized regular study sessions with friends for subjects that usually drove them buggy. Group studying can make some assignments seem less boring and can be a great fog clearer, too. "In a group of people, chances are at least one person will know how to do the hard problems," said Jill. Her friends wouldn't do the work *for* her. But they'd offer each other friendly suggestions if one of them got fogged up. Explaining a tricky problem to a friend can help you learn it even better. Yolanda pointed out another advantage to group studying: "If I missed something in class, I could get it from my friends."

GRIPE #10
TEST JITTERS

Save your jamming and slamming for basketball. Here are less nerve-rattling ways to gear up for quizzes and tests.

TIME TRAVEL

Hop in your time machine and travel forward in time to test day. Imagine yourself staring at the test. What kind of questions are on it? If you haven't a clue, you better travel back in time—way back—to revisit all those class discussions of the past few weeks. "Try to remember the points the teacher spent a lot of time on or tried to emphasize," said Peggy. "Those will probably show up on the test." Some precious documents you have in your possession can also give you a clue as to what will be on the test. For starters, there's your textbook. The end-of-chapter questions may put in a test appearance. So might the kinds of questions you've done recently for homework.

Just to be sure, zoom up to the present. "Ask the teacher what type of test it will be and what will be covered," said Meredith. Then you'll know for sure what to go over as you study.

EARLY BIRD

Of course, by keeping up with the homework, you've already learned a lot of the stuff that will be on the test. But it's smart to review everything that will be covered. The sooner you start, the better, said our teen advisers. Waiting to pull a last-minute cram session was *not* high on their list of super study skills. Charay's tip: "Begin studying two or three days before the test. You can jot down questions you don't understand and have time to ask the teacher about them before the test."

PLAN OF ATTACK

Okay, so you're ready to start gearing up for the big "T." Where to start? Our test-studying whizzes generally followed Laura's plan of attack: "Look over all the notes you took." That includes notes from class as well as reading notes. Several teens would use a marker to highlight important points in their notes. Many would also read through the textbook chapter again and try to answer the questions at the end of the chapter.

Next point of attack? Old homework. Many students would redo some problems from recent assignments, just to be sure they really were on top of things. If there's a part you don't know, review it some more. "Spend more time going over the stuff you *don't* know than stuff you do know," said Loretta.

To learn stuff they were still fuzzy on, the teens would use some of the memory-boosting tricks described back on pages 23 to 29.

WRITE ON (and on and on ...)

Just *looking* over their notes before a test wasn't enough for many of our study specialists. "Sometimes I'd completely rewrite all my notes while I was studying," explained Kelsey. "That way I'd remember them

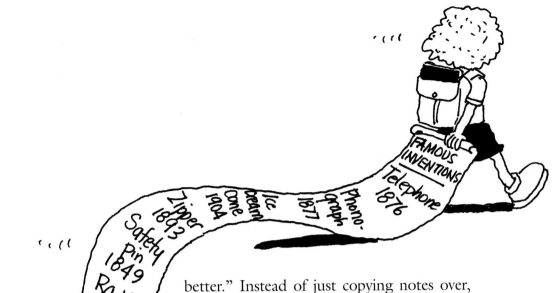

better." Instead of just copying notes over, Sarah would "rewrite notes in my own words so I'd understand them." Others would put the information into diagrams or charts. Andrew's write-on approach: He'd try to write everything he needed to know for a test on one sheet of paper. He'd carry it around all day and look at it when he had time.

Other teens went list crazy. They'd make lists of dates, vocabulary words, and important people or events that might put in a test appearance. Many used the two-column approach, putting the event or date in the left-hand column and the explanation in the right-hand column. Then they could fold the paper in half to see how much they remembered.

QUIZ KIDS

As they reached the final countdown to test day, many teens would take a trial run through the test. No, they wouldn't get their hands on the real test in advance. Instead, they'd make up their own pretend version of it. For spelling tests, all they had to do was round up a par-

ent or friend to read out the spelling list for the student to write down. Coming up with a pretend test for other subjects took a bit more effort. "I'd write out sample questions that might be on the test," said Kelsey. "I'd also write the answers." Then she could cover up the answers to quiz herself, or have a parent quiz her.

Others would trade pretend tests with a friend, to see how high they'd score on their buddy's made-up test. Lester and his friends used a different approach. "We'd take turns quizzing each other on topics that might be on the test," he explained.

Group studying for tests was popular with many of our homework aces. Some would try to lighten up these study sessions by playing games like Jeopardy with information they had to learn. Elisabeth and her friends made up silly stories with information that would be on the test. "When we took the test," she said, "we remembered the information because of those silly stories."

GOOD NIGHT

"Know when to stop studying," advised Christine. "If you're tired and have been studying a lot for a test, quit. Go to sleep. Don't over-cram or you'll panic."

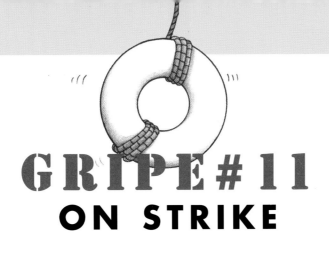

GRIPE #11
ON STRIKE

Some days, even the high-achieving, super high school juniors and seniors who've been sharing their study tips all through this book felt just like the kid in this cartoon. So what did they do?

NO SWEAT

When Roger got the urge to go "on strike," that's just what he'd do—he'd slam shut his books, flop out, and take a short nap. Others would head off and do something fun for a while. "I'd take it easy," said Linh. "I knew I'd get the work done. So I'd take a breather and return when I felt ready."

Some teens admitted that after taking a "breather," they often had to force themselves to get back to work, especially on a gorgeous day. For those hard-to-start-studying days, try Kimberly's advice. "Don't get in a rut," Kimberly said. "Sometimes a change can help. Do your homework someplace different—at the library or a friend's house."

What if you slip up and don't quite get all the homework done? "Don't worry too much," said Rusty. "You'll still live." Work faster the next day and catch up.

WHAT'S THE POINT?

"Homework can be a pain at times," said Alisha, "but I've learned a lot by doing it." Amber explained that "it sort of pounds the stuff into your head."

The teens noted other good points to doing homework. You don't have to study so hard at test time since you'll already know the material. Plus, doing homework can make sitting in class more fun because you'll know what everyone else is talking about and can join in instead of zone out.

Benjamin noted another good point: "The more homework you do, the more you learn." True, and the better you'll tend to do in school. Educators have found that the more time kids spend on homework, the better their grades.

"Don't let homework ruin your life," said Kathy. It hasn't ruined hers. By sharing so many super study tips in this book, Kathy and our other teen advisers have done their best to keep homework from being a hassle for *you*. Her last bit of advice: "Don't forget to have fun, too."

A FINAL WORD
ABOUT THE TEEN ADVISERS

The 300 high school juniors and seniors who filled out questionnaires for this book came from all over the United States. Most were members of their school's honor society. The stars on the map on page 76 show where their schools were located.

The author would like to give a big thank you to all the students who filled out questionnaires and to the following teachers and administrators who arranged for students to take part in this project: Ms. Sharon Brown, Kirtland Central High School, Kirtland, NM; Mr. Thomas R. Coupe, Jerome High School, Jerome, ID; Mr. David W. Ehrich, James A. Garfield High School, Seattle, WA; Ms. Sheila Foley, White Plains Youth Bureau, White Plains, NY; Ms. Sandy Fritz, Bettendorf High School, Bettendorf, IA; Mrs. Bonnie Fullmer, Centennial High School, Meridian, ID; Ms. Barbara A. Golaski, Western High School, Baltimore, MD; Ms. Drema C. Green, Greenbrier West High School, Charmco, WV; Ms. Barbara Greenberg, Ridgewood Preparatory School, Metairie, LA; Mrs. Linda Hoenstine, Dr. Phillips High School, Orlando, FL; Mrs. Cheryl Kothe, Washington Park Senior High School, Racine, WI; Mrs. Bonnie S. Maddox, Capital High School, Charleston, WV; Ms. Susan Meeker,

WHERE OUR TEEN ADVISERS CAME FROM

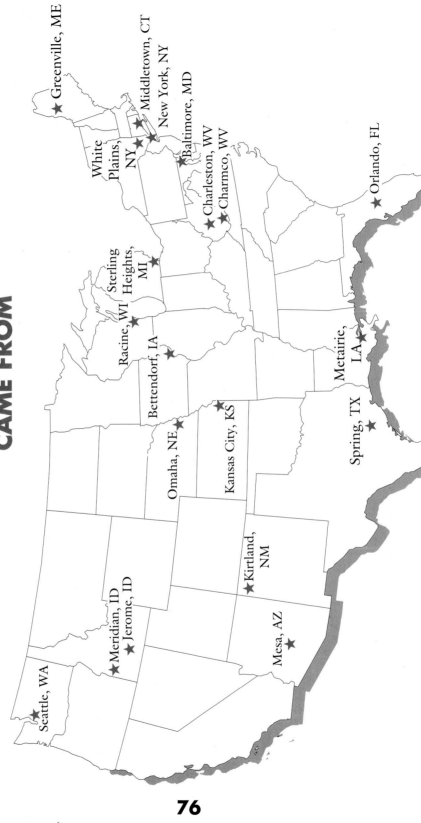

Greenville, ME

Middletown, CT

New York, NY

Baltimore, MD

White Plains, NY

Charleston, WV

Charmco, WV

Orlando, FL

Sterling Heights, MI

Racine, WI

Metairie, LA

Bettendorf, IA

Kansas City, KS

Spring, TX

Omaha, NE

Kirtland, NM

Meridian, ID

Jerome, ID

Mesa, AZ

Seattle, WA

Hunter College High School, New York, NY; Mr. John Montemerlo, Xavier High School, Middletown, CT; Mr. William S. Nelson, Westside High School, Omaha, NE; Ms. Stella R. Ollarsaba, Dobson High School, Mesa, AZ; Mr. Ron R. Pelletier, Greenville High School, Greenville, ME; Ms. Nancy M. Smith, Klein Oak High School, Spring, TX; Mr. Robert Van Camp, Henry Ford II High School, Sterling Heights, MI; Ms. Phyllis Whiteside, J.C. Harmon High School, Kansas City, KS.

Thanks also to the following who arranged for their fourth through eighth graders to tell about their homework gripes: Mr. Jeff Cohen, P.S. 29, Brooklyn, NY; Ms. Pat French, Saints Simon and Jude Elementary School, Louisville, KY; Ms. Debbie Henthorn, Hayfield Secondary School, Alexandria, VA; Mr. Herb Hinz, Ebeling-Utica Schools, Mt. Clemens, MI. For helpful advice, thanks also go to Professor Cindy I. Carlson, Department of Educational Psychology, University of Texas; and Professor Tim Keith, Division of School Psychology, Alfred University, Alfred, NY.

INDEX